thoughts of Ray THE SEQUEL

published by:
DeeClare Publishing, LLC
Indianapolis IN

The Thoughts of Ray, the Sequel is a compilation of the author's thoughts expressed through poetry — Ray's love language. He shares his gift of creative speech in a very unique way and each piece is a literary segment of the author's journey that emerges from the depths of his soul.

Author:	Thomas Ray
Cover Design | Typeset:	Deesignz Web & Graphics Studio
Interpretive Editorial:	Deneen G. Matthews
Categories:	Poetry, Fiction, Autobiography, Faith, Spirituality, Inspiration, Social Advocacy
ISBN:	978-0-578-91398-8

Printed in the United States of America
Paperback, 104 pages

table of contents

remarks

"After reading this unselfish self-journey by Tom Ray, what seemed to be a dystopian society that we presently live, doesn't feel so perilous. Brother Ray's keen observations and reactions to them are best displayed in this thought-provoking, spiritually uplifting, and often humorous piece of work. Tom Ray, thank you for selflessly sharing your inner journey, so that we can learn to enjoy and soldier through ours." Peace! — Tom E. Morgan

"First, it is my honor to comment on the words from the heart and soul from friend and brother, Tom Ray. You are a reflection of God's light. Bringing forth the positive words of power to a society that is bent on destruction – you are able to see and be the balance – the positive. Everybody knows there are two sides to reality –one negative and one positive – keep it positive; that's the side that our ancestors are on, and we shall overcome if we allow our minds to be renewed by the Spirit of God and the principles of God that are universal and natural. Words are power. Continue letting the people know that we all got power – what are we going to use it for? Good or Evil? Either we are part of the problem or part of the solution. Thanks, Bro. Tom, for being part of the solution! Uplifting the best of our Culture. Ase, Ase, Ase."— Baaba O, Aka Bro. Rob

"Telling his story through his P.A.I.N., Tom Ray gives an honest account of memories, love & life. Each passage gives light to every experience. He uses his unique voice and style to share the ride of highs, lows, failures, and triumphs through P.A.I.N. and spreads love. Thank you for your story." — T. Bridgewater

"Poetic artistry with his own soulful flava! Ray exercises his unique mastery of words, phrases, and sound bites to frame the phases of his life and shape the stages of his journey. He invites us to engage and interpret the whole while serving up palatable portions for the reader to ponder. While we laugh, reminisce, and relate with Ray, forehead wrinkles form and serve as indicators of thought-provoking content in direct context with his life." — D. Matthews

everyone needs a change of direction — that change requires making a choice!

Change,

To convert or transform,

Is a vital outcome in the improvement of self —

How we put on new form.

A change of life perspective,

A change of setting, of mind and diet;

Of trials and tribulations to triumph!

Change to be perfect will only taunt us;

Yet will occur when we renew our minds by the word of God,

And put into action what He taught us.

Let's upgrade our life testimony

And do our part to effect change in this world;

By renewing ourselves;

Then and only then

Can the matters at hand take a better turn.

If you desire change, it begins with you.

To see a difference in the current state of our society,

Change your vibration too.

Change emerges even in the midst of tragedy,

And will either unite us or divide us

During these tough times we are encountering.

Change is inevitable.

Change is here!

Time to put on the whole armor of God

And do your share.

We all have a purpose and assignment to accomplish. If you are reading this, then your breathing wish — should be to make every living situation better. While strange it may feel, the need for change is very real; and what we can't do alone, we must do together!

Now —

Stop feeding the lies.

Stop fueling the fears,

Insecurities and made-up thoughts;

And feed your mind

Food that is divine

Minus the genetically modified

GMO.

Any negative vibes in your aura,

You got to let go

When you want to grow.

Whatever got you in bondage —

You got to let it go.

These aren't just some words that sound good.

This is what I know,

What I've been through,
Getting through;
What you going through
Isn't anything new;
And old ways
Won't open up
New doors.
Let go.
You got to!

change

Change starts with you!
Change in you, literally;
A complete renewed spirit,
Far from perfect.
Beloved,
Every step you take
Through your journey
Is well worth it.
You got purpose.
The victory is yours.
Claim it.
You deserve it.
LOVE *

the thoughts of ray — the sequel

Blessings to the world;

Blessings to our little boys and girls,

Blessings.

Bless the water;

Bless Flint Michigan;

And everybody reading this.

Father, Bless America.

You know we got some issues that need to be dealt with;

And your power is the greatest.

So I give you the glory,

The Narrator of this story.

You know every word written

'Cause they come from you.

We need to seek you

Because everything else is see-through.

Now —

Stomp on them demons

That's beneath you.

BLESSINGS!

Heavenly Father — our Creator, I write these words to glorify your divine name to praise you and thank you. We thank you for the angels who encamp about us and for our ancestors who have paved the way before us.

I ask that you continue to do your divine work in me and forgive every one of us for the sins we commit; and I thank you for doing so by your merciful grace.

Father, bless this day that you have made; bless everything my heart desires because you know it best. Bless everyone I encounter from this day forward; and bless everyone who has impacted my life in the past and present. I love you all like God loves you. Love is love and God is love.

I pray that our divine healer will bless us all with good health, wisdom and wealth. I pray that every household is blessed with all its needs and wants. Bless every parent and child worldwide. Bless us all, God.

Bless every acre of your land struck by natural disasters. Bless my family and all my brothers and sisters. Bless us all to continue in all we do because everything is working for your good to be made manifest.

God bless everyone reading this prayer and all those who are blind who need to hear this prayer. Touch every mind and heart and draw us closer to you. I thank you unconditionally for every miracle and for the life of your Son you sacrificed for us to live in the abundance of joy and peace. I give thanks for all you do, all you have done, and for every word there is to come. In the name and under the authority of your Son, Jesus Christ, our Lord and Savior we pray, Amen.

You Ready?

Many years before we were born, our ancestors in Africa communicated in a very unique fashion. My favorite instrument, the drum, comes in many types, shapes and sizes — the Conga, Djembe, Tar, Ashiko and Base; while the beat of the drum creates an orchestra of different thumps and echoes that we move, groove, create dialect and formulate libation to.

Vibrations of the drum can touch the depths of the soul, and shake us and awaken us to our authentic personas. From the sound of the drum evolves music, and **MUSIC IS LIFE!**

Music is an element of life that connects us all and purposes to inspire. Organic vibes consistent with what we feel, not what is manufactured according to industry standard. Music is a reflection of who we are; and its origins usually trace back to our generational ties. While good music is healing for the spirit and elevates us higher, great music is why new skool samples ole skool with no skool rules that compel us to compose the music we're supposed to.

What would life be without music? I'll let you think that through…

music is life

Music is life.

Well, I definitely need it to function.

I'll be the first to say

I can't go a day

Without listening to some Marvin Gaye.

That good music —

It makes you move when you groove to it;

And the content is nowhere next to nonsense;

I'll testify,

And it isn't hard to tell

When you got common sense.

If you can't feel it,

Then it's not real;

The energy's not right.

It doesn't sit right on you

If it doesn't grow on you.

Music is a necessity.

We move to the beat of the drum.

Babies are made from music;

So can we go Half on a Baby,

Sweet lady?

Most importantly,

It makes you feel good

When it touches your soul;

Harmony is deeper than you know.

It turns Boys to Men,

And a female with dreams into a Destiny's Child.

Bigger than life —

Music will change your whole family's life;

And it impacts the world more

When there's a message to it;

Whether its rhythm 'n blues or hip hop —

I prefer ole skool,

The new jack swing era,

Or the golden era.

A lot of this new music is straight up garbage.

The corporate devils got their hands in it now,

And the radio is just a headache

Playing the same songs

Over and over.

It used to be a form of communication

We desired for;

Now DJs are getting fired for

Not playing the same ole stuff.

A lot of these so-called rappers are saying the

Same old stuff,

Like I got this and I got that;

Well I know what I got;

I got Brown Sugar on my playlist,

The Notorious B.I.G.,

Da Brat, I'm so Funkdafied,

DMX,

Yeah, you can Get At Me Dog,

I'm ready to Get It On

Anytime

Like Marvin

With a female I just met named Bonita Applebum.

She's got the 411 like Mary,

And I let her share my world.

I told her

I'm a ruff neck who Don't Believe the Hype;

I'm similar to a Public Enemy.

My older brother calls me Hammer

To this day,

So you know you Can't Touch This!

I does this,

I am this,

I live this,

I ssshhh this;

And it stink like Funk Doctor Spot;

And I Bring the Pain like Meth.

I'm So So Def without the chain, sincerely;

I hope you get my point of view clearly.

This real music;

I'm a seed from that era;

My soul glows because of that era.

Music like that will make you dance.

Where you at?

No matter if you White or Black

And, oh yeah, rest in peace to the King of Pop,

Michael Jack,

James Brown,

2 Pac,

Heavy D —

You know I got Nuttin' But Love for you;

And I Ain't Half Stepping.

This thing here is deeper

Then All About the Benjamins.

It will take you to your Ecstasy

When there is a love for it —

Music that is —

It's my life, I need it;

If I was lying in a hospital bed,

It will be my IV;

And a big shout to all the DJs;

Funkmaster Flex,

Kid Capri,

And can't forget about Ron G

And all the pioneers.

Music has been a part of my life

All thirty plus years,

And I refuse to let it go.

We are one;

It's Electric!

It calms your soul as soon as things get hectic,

And you know it's therapeutic,

So once it gets staticky,

Your best bet is to mute it;

And we all know it's universal.

So no matter where you're from

Or your ethnicity,

We can all relate when it's authentic;

And God didn't make no mistake

With His influence on the Human Beat Box.

He showed us

We can make music on our own

On Yo! MTV Raps;

And if someone told you music ain't life,

They lied to you, Jack.

Real hip hop,

They say it died,

But there is

Life after death.

So to all my real music lovers,

Let's bring it back…

And that's a Rap!

And that's a fact.

Let's bring it back!

MUSIC IS LIFE (YouTube, Tom Ray, Music Is Life)

Growing up, I was exposed to soulful music with meaningful content — the kind of music that made you dance. Oh, and let's take a moment to reminisce ole skool hip hop!

I love music, point blank, period. Who doesn't? It's therapeutic, and when the vibrations are right, my ear can't help but to tune in to it.

Don't get me wrong; I have nothing against this modern age of music. I only pray that artists dig deeper and produce good music —timeless hits — or I'm afraid it won't last long.

I salute every artist of all genres and forms. We were created to stir up amazing portraits of artistic expression. Made in the design of our Creator, should we not create? Our passions are used to invent the art that we portray to the audience of the world and await acknowledgment that they can relate. There's no need to copy or imitate. Be unique. Be content to be wonderfully fashioned to accomplish God's purpose. On the level beneath the surface usually lie the answers long sought for.

Develop your talents and gifts; become your passion and choose from an endless list of possibilities. Put your hands to the work, give it one hundred percent, and watch God bless the fruit of your labor and cause the work of your hands to prosper in it.

Peace.

Message: *God works with us and empowers us when we are willing to do the inward work. He also desires to bless us so that we can become a blessing to others. We should pray for one another, love our neighbor, and be true to our neighbor even when it hurts.*

Sometimes truth hurts, but it will also set us free. Truth is knowledge and applied knowledge produces wisdom. Wisdom is a gift from God that empowers and equips us. When we silence our voices, His becomes distinct; and He will direct our way and teach us how to walk in greater freedom and revelation.

silence is golden

Silence is golden;

Well,

I don't have much to say

'Cause you can say

So much

In a short convo — pronto.

Words are powerful,

And faith really moves mountains.

Now, that's a spiritual jewel

That comes true

When you choose to believe.

Now plant your mustards seeds

And water them, see?

That's the thing about flowers;

They take time to blossom

With plenty of sunlight.

SO, SHINE BELOVED

Once your light starts to glow

And you begin to radiate.

stand up

And brace yourself for the fall.
If you do,
Just get right back up
And stay in pursuit,
And gather your troops;
There's strength in numbers.
Just subtract the egos
And add the confidence;
Divide the unity all over.
Love is always the answer,
Don't let anyone tell you different.
We all the same to one God;
Lucifer will make you think otherwise.
You and me,
We come from
A greater tribe,
While this world is in dying need
Of good vibes and creative minds.
Special shout to my Harlem kinfolk.
You'll be amazed how my pen stroke
 Can manifest vivid pictures
That you can feel;
Visionaries

Know the deal.

If you can see it,

You can be it.

It just takes hard work

To achieve it.

This world is ours

And you best believe it.

That's the only way we are going to make it —

When we believe.

Faith is the number one element we need

To proceed,

And it don't stop

When you're on a mission fueled by

P.A.I.N (Progress after its Nemesis).

If you are sitting down

In the midst of all we are going through,

What do you have to gain?

So stand up for something

And be sturdy about it,

And look down

Only on those who you are picking up.

Together we can make it.

In God I trust;

All we got

Is us.

Just remember this;
Ain't no Captain America
Coming to save us!
Don't get it twisted,
It's on us to
Stand up.

STAND UP! (YouTube, Tom Ray, Stand Up)

The Thoughts of Ray, The Sequel —

When I put the pen to the page,
I'm dropping gems, jewels,
And food for your mind.
So, are you hungry,
And are you ready to shine, beloved?
The words I write,
I give you my word,
You gon' love them,
And I mean that.
Death in the palms of my hands;
I really seen that.
So, making it out the hood one day,
I really dream that;
And now I'm focusing on
Dream catching.

No, I'm not perfect.
I still love all my imperfections.
You can hear the truth
In all my confessions;
Because I was taught
Why lie when the truth will
Set you free?
When you look in the mirror,
Do you know what you see?
Now that's something
You got to deal with,
And that's real talk.
The only time you fail in life
Is when you quit,
So keep pushing.
It gets greater later,
And hard times
Become even better
When you trust in our Lord and Savior
Or whomever you pray to.
God deserves all prayers due,
For all He has brought you through.
And don't get me wrong;
I am not preaching;
I'm just speaking from the heart;

Giving light to dark,

Passing out gems so we all shine.

I got no problem with showing love;

You want some?

I know you tired of the hate.

I got love for everybody;

I even love your whole family.

Now run tell that and take notes

From some of my realest words ever wrote!

speaking from the heart

In my 30 plus years on this earth, writing has influenced my life in so many ways. Ever since I picked up a pen back in 2005, through writing I learned the power of words and manifestation that accompanies them. Transcribing my journey has also become therapy and a source of comfort to combat my own personal life struggles.

God has blessed me with this artistic gift, and it has become my choice of self-expression. I believe that writing can contribute to healing when thoughts unseen are captured and transferred onto paper. Even when it seems no one is listening, writing can become an outlet to help organize and navigate through life variables to find or rediscover meaning.

Message: *The life we live all began with God's word, and all things are possible through Him, beloved. Scripture instructs us* *to write the vision. Seek God for His purpose for your life; write down your goals and desires and commit them to prayer. You'll have to be patient and watch God, in His perfect timing, bring to pass the vision in line with His perfect plan.*

Time is precious, so the question at hand is, what are you doing with your time?

i got a question

Question —

Did you realize yet

It's the small things

That count, Cuz?

And I call you Cuz

Because we all family in God's eyes;

And besides,

When you pull up to the cookout

And you don't know anyone,

Whose name you call,

Cousin Pete?

I guarantee you gon' eat.

This is that poetic justice, off beat,

With a whole lot of love

To make my words complete.

They're connected to the higher power,

So you gon' feel this.

I'll have your appetite satisfied

Off this food for thought.

Come and get your brain food.

I'm student of life,

So I stay

In school,

Trying to learn something new.

Come to class, beloved.

The master teacher appears

When the student wants to learn.

Remove the L,

Then you earn.

Right now, it's our turn.

Go and get what you want, beloved.

(See, right now is the time for triumph and victory!)

Something we are all striving to obtain

And succeed at in life.

Live up to your destiny;

What God has called you to be.

Be that king,

Be that queen,

Be more than the eyes can see.

Be more than just the book,

Be the read.

Be the one who feeds,

Not the one

Who is all about greed.

By giving,

You'll get more

Because of the seeds you planted to receive.

Trust and believe even when you can't see.

Know that your faith is the first step,

So get ready.

You must get rid of the

Heavy burden you carry,

And I know it might seem scary

Letting go of something you thought you need;

When in fact,

It's something that made you bleed;

Brought you down to your knees

Asking and begging,

Saying things like

Lord, please

Grant me triumph,

Give me victory;

You will get all the praise and glory!

Lord, can you hear me?

Help me out this muck and miry clay.

First, you must be willing to go the divine way

And listen to all the Holy Ghost has to say.

God said, "Don't run.

Don't walk.

Don't sit.

Just stand still

And don't sway."

Just trust in God,

And God will

Make a way out of no way!

written by
Someone I call Mr. President — J. J. Simmons

* * * * * *

You see, we follow the Creator's order. It's honorable to give credit where credit is due. Recognizing the gift in someone else allows them to shine and casts a greater light upon mankind. Who better than family?

Thank you, Cousin.

— Ray

The Thoughts of Ray, The Sequel —

In order for us to experience true victory, we must be on one accord. It's time to start love all over and get back to the basics.

Why is it so hard for us to come together in unison?

Is it ego?

Hate for one another's race?

Or are we just too selfish?

When truly we better together,

You know?

Unity is our oppressor's

Worst nightmare;

And instead,

We become a part of the nightmare,

Killing each other, hating each other,

While forgetting to love one another.

See?

Love is the strongest vibration

To spark change;

And without it,

Life will always remain the same.

Standing by graveyards,

Releasing tears of pain,

When it should be tears of joy,

While standing at the mountain top,

Holding hands,

Praising the Almighty, man,

Who truly understands

Unity is key.

Only thing is

Getting all of us to believe in...

unity

Internalize this —

United we stand, divided we fall! In order to mend this chaos, we must stand tall, do the right thing, and start taking responsibility for the choices we make. Selfish ways won't cut it, and by helping someone else, we help better ourselves. Lend a helping hand and become great through service. But... if service is beneath you, leadership is beyond you!

Peace.

Follow the leader,

Leader,

Leader,

Follow the leader.

Follow the leader,

Leader,

Leader.

Wait.

Hold up!

Are we supposed to follow the leader

Or follow Gods order?

An authentic leader will show

Others how to lead

And create their own path,

Rather than being followed

By false duplication.

A true leader shows others

The way that leads to more leaders.

Every one of us has the capability

To lead;

Instead,

We look at man or woman for validation,

Assuming others' lives is better than our own;

When we all been blessed to be great

And leave a major impact on this earth's surface.

So go ahead and throw that

Capital L on your chest

And lead, loved one!

follow the leader

Now let that marinate as I...

invite you into freedom

You have been selected to experience
The liberty of freedom;
You are invited into the house of love.
Kick your shoes off,
Get comfortable.
Mi casa es su casa,
Let's break bread,
Turning one loaf into plenty
So everyone gets fed.
We gon' eat,
I just pray you don't get greedy
Or selfish.
I pray you make it to the table
So you could take part in the feast,
'Cause it's real in the field.
You might not make it home
And home is where the heart is.
What is your heart filled with?
Love or hate?
Faith or hopelessness?
Gems or fossils?
Whatever's on your mind
That you are striving for is highly possible

To manifest.

That's all truth;

I'll be the first to confess.

Freedom is free indeed;

You are allowed to be

Who you are

In the house of liberty.

It's a judge-free zone

Governed by knowledge of self

With the power to act

As one wants

Without hindrance or restraint.

We are free at last,

Free at last!

Thank God Almighty,

We are free at last!

In this experience called life, we all exercise our freedom to believe what we want to believe. God's laws undergird my system of belief, and His liberty extends beyond infinity, beloved one. I'm certain of it. That freedom doesn't cost a thing monetarily, but your free will of choice is required.

Peace.

The Thoughts of Ray, The Sequel —

As we embark upon the journey to freedom and search for true liberty, "flaws" appear and self-hate poses as an enemy to the mind, body, and soul. Our weaknesses and shortcomings bring light to hidden insecurities and frustrate the illusion of flawless perfection. We should make note that there is not a single unblemished soul on this earth.

Even portraits painted by the hand of renowned artists and showcased as perfect works of art have slight imperfections undetected by the untrained eye and only known to the artist.

Oftentimes, our own flaws go unnoticed by others but are there as catalysts for our growth. Embrace them. As a matter of fact, love and appreciate that they are a part of our unique genetic makeup and contribute to and challenge the process of who we are becoming.

Your image

Is how God created you!

Whether big or small,

Thin or thick;

Listen family,

Build your foundation brick by brick.

The pyramids weren't built in a day;

And believe it or not,

They're not one hundred percent perfect.

They're wonderfully made to the Creator's eye

And well worth it.

Your inner peace —

You deserve it!

So don't waste your time

Trying to be perfect or

flawless

Seek greatness because you are GREAT! Created in the image of excellence, make no mistake; you are who God made you to be. You are made marvelously through His power and majesty. Make no doubt about it; speak life and prosperity. Align your life with His will and watch the power of words and your diligent labor transform your entire existence. As a man thinks in his heart, so is he!

Good thoughts feel good

When you say it.

Now say, I feel good,

And experience the power of words.

If you are looking for instant gratification,

Know it doesn't work

Like that.

It takes practice and belief

Because words have so much power

That

You can speak God's desires into existence,

Or speak death into your present.

There is mighty power in the tongue,

So pay close attention to what you say.

Think before every word you speak;

Practice what you preach,

Because if your words don't match your actions,

Your words become worthless.

Now say what you mean

And mean what you say;

If you don't have anything nice to say,

Don't say anything at all.

You have two ears and one mouth

For a reason, Beloved.

Listen to the calm voices in your head

And don't listen to

Someone telling you

You cannot do something —

the power of words

Before you continue, I'd like to express my love for you and yours and my sincerest gratitude for your continuous support. I pray that you prosper in all the good you aspire to do and experience an abundance of true happiness. May God bless you to enjoy the life He's given you!

Yours truly,

Tom Ray

SUCCESS IS THE MISSION!!!

psa

I've been blessed to give back to my community and use my socially relevant spoken words to encourage my brothers and sisters to seek enlightenment, healing, and God-inspired love. History provides accounts of historians who influenced masses of people and how some excelled as a result. I pay homage to every humanitarian who passed on the knowledge and wisdom they received, while remaining devoted to uplift spirits and replicate the model of "Each one teach one."

As I step into my calling as an inspirational poet, spoken word artist, educator, and author, I readily assume responsibility to bestow benevolence upon my community and the world at large and share the knowledge I gain to encourage and elevate the minds of my fellow man to seek true knowledge of self. I realize on this journey that my purpose is beyond me and that one of the greatest things I can achieve in this life is to help someone else live up to their maximum destined potential. I fully acknowledge that I am here to live out my life assignment and inspire, spread love, and uplift my people.

who am i?

A golden, imperfect,
Spiritual being
Created in the image of greatness.
I am also
An image of black power,
Black love,

Black strength,

Black excellence,

And the list goes down the line.

Rosetta Simmons is the structure

Of my spine.

She is my backbone

My everything!

And my FAMILY MEANS

THE WORLD TO ME...

I wouldn't be here

If it wasn't for y'all;

I appreciate each and every one of y'all.

We are one;

We are love;

I am love;

I am a soldier,

A warrior,

My brother's keeper,

A creative creator,

An elevator,

A motivator,

Educator,

A trendsetter;

A go-getter

Who knows better,

So I will do better.
I am an author,
A poet,
A king,
An all-around cool
Human being.
I am the representation
Of my ancestors' prayers,
And I am a mediator
Of my peers;
And I am blessed to be here.
I am Yonkers.
I am Tom Ray, Jr.
I am the future.
I am the power of love.
R.I.P. to Luther!
I am not the product of my environment.
I am royal.
I am Africa.
I am here for you.
I am all that I say I am.
There is more to me
Than what you see.
I am truth.

Self-awareness, self-love, and self-determination are key factors to living an abundant life. Identity births forth confidence. Claim your greatness. Speak positivity over your life. What we think, we become; and what we know, we stand firmly on; and no one can dissuade us.

History has proven that we originate from excellence. We are royalty and have resilient energy. Study our ancestry; therein lies the evidence. We are intellectuals, authors, artists, pillars of strength, movers and shakers, and the blueprint of culture.

Simply put, we are it!

We are teachers, leaders, natural-born healers, polymaths, innovators, and inventors. We are more than just the next athlete or MC and much more than eyes can see. In a world full of endless possibilities, we can be all we want to be when we embrace our true identity.

Commit it to memory, this is a divine message from the Great I Am; and remember, I am exactly who I say I am. Question is — who are you?

The Thoughts of Ray, The Sequel —

Family, I hope thus far you have gained some food for thought from my thought-filled expressions of inspiration and encouragement. These are the continuation of *The Thoughts of Ray, from My Heart to Yours*, and I pray you enjoy the message.

If you would like to offer feedback, comments, or inquiry, please feel free to reach out to me via **email @ thomasray156@yahoo.** com, or on social media — **Facebook @TomRay** or **Instagram @trdatsit.**

Now, a great segue to the next poem entitled…

facebook status

Yes,

I'm talented with this gift

I have been blessed with;

That's already been established.

Truth be told,

You will never know

What's on my mind,

Even if you read my Facebook status.

I'm a step ahead,

And I don't know much.

I speak when spoken to

Or when the energy is right.

Other than that,

I keep my mouth shut

And eyes wide open

'Cause there's no sleeping

In the wild jungle.

We still got dreams,

Though

Deny the fulfillment.

Do nonsense,

And senseless acts,

Hate crimes;

And Satan's temptation

Is in control

Of all that.

His manipulation

Is a complete lie,

So keep your head

Held high through that

Gray sky

Until you see the light—

It's up there.

Find your

True self

And stay grounded in a spiritual foundation;

And a word to the wise,

Lay off the PlayStation

Because life isn't a Gameboy;

The picture

Bigger than that TV frame, boy.

So think big,

As big as you want;

You can only stop you.

Adversity is unstoppable;

You are going to face it,

And when you do,

You might as well embrace it,

Because there is no

Erasing it.

It's permanent in this life we live;

Our story is already written.

So,

Fulfill your destiny,

Take control of your legacy,

Say a prayer for your enemies

Because it's spiritual warfare,

While mine is in the hood

Fighting for welfare;

We can't get healthcare,

And the cops just don't care.

We on our own —

Brainwashed and killing each other.

Take a second to think about this…

The crime rate is up

And the brutality rate is up.

Love is the answer

And there isn't enough!

We the solution though,

So keep your faith, son.

Don't be good,

Be great, son.

We all different,

And still we relate —

Done!

Peace.

While we aim to connect with one another, chaos creeps in to divide us. The chaos serves a purpose, however, because all things are still working together for our good.

So, with all this

chaos

In the world,

It's got me praying for our little boys and girls.

Situations are getting real,

And body parts are getting fake;

Fear is in the place of faith.

Our new president is a snake,

With funerals popping up daily,

And families

Can barely pay for the wake.

Wait!

That's not the half —

These young thugs

Claim

It's all about the money
And don't even know how to add;
Always skipping class
And pants hanging off their ass.
They need an ass whipping —
With years of no discipline,
Now they crippling.
It's the way of the world,
Truthfully.
It's a systematic project,
And we the pawns in the process
Until we wake up.
We're in the age of information,
And the young world
Don't even care to attend
A graduation.
I'm steady praying for change
And displaying it.
There's only one life to live;
There's no replacing;
And tomorrow ain't
Promised.
That's a friendly reminder —
You better embrace this moment.

You're blessed

When you got clothes on your back,

Food on your table,

And a roof over your head to go with it.

Now I'm 'a leave with

Some words to go home with,

Get your temple right —

Mind,

Body,

And soul.

The younger generation

Looking for love; that's why

They are out of control;

Some of these grown folks too.

Lend a helping hand,

Reach one and teach one.

The greatest thing you can do in life

Is by helping another

And loving thyself

Before you call yourself

Loving another.

There is no future in fronting;

You only playing yourself

When you call yourself

Stunting.

Let God

Lead you where He designed

You to go.

You will be lost

On your own understanding.

So stand on your ten toes

With your head in the air;

Fill your heart with love,

And stop fueling the fear;

And in the mist of all the madness,

Get closer to God,

Because the Creator will always be there.

Vibrate higher

And stay away from the chaos!

An essential element in life to combat chaos, keep the balance, and ward off strife is positive energy!

positive energy

If there is anything

I ask for,

That's just it,

Positive energy —

I need it,

I'm addicted to it,

I shoot it in my veins;

You can have a hit.

The needle clean

And full of good spirits,

So let's get high off

Love and flavor vibes

And show gratitude towards one another

Everyday;

Not just on birthdays.

Positive energy

Makes you feel good and comfortable.

Positive energy

Is what the world needs more of.

Negative energy is its opponent.

That good energy wins the battle every time

Because love always overpowers the hate,

And love is the father of positive energy.

So how you like that?

I love it

As you should.

Positive energy

Clears up all static;

It also keeps you grounded in this

Corrupt world.

It's truly imperative for

Our little boys and girls

In this angry world.

In closing,

When you are filled

With more positive energy

Than negative,

You will see doors open in your life

You have never imagined,

And the blessings will overflow

All due to dope vibes!

In life, there's always a positive and negative to everything; as well as two sides to every story. A healthy balance is necessary to keep you steadfast throughout your journey.

balance

Balance is key;

Not only is it major.

Balance lets you know

Where things stand.

The first two assets

On the balance beam are

Love and hate,

And love overpowers the hate by twos.

People just love to hate

And don't have a clue what they are doing,

Inspired by subconscious self-hate.

Then there's good and bad,

Right from wrong,

Women vs. men,

And we need each other

To reproduce life.

We come from women, fellas,

And women come from man.

So you tell me,

Who's more important?

Truthfully,

Both male and female

Are a necessity

To the balance of life.

We both make mistakes

That teach life lessons.

Now you got

Lessons vs. blessings.

At the end of the day

Lessons start and finish as blessings.

Also,

You can either

Tell the truth or a lie

During a confession.

You make the choice —

To be artificial or authentic,

Because the truth will set you free,

And living a lie

Will leave you sitting

Behind bars

In a penitentiary;

Which leads to

Freedom vs. enslavement,

Darkness vs. enlightenment,

Knowledge as opposed to mis-education,

Divine praising,

Overshadowing Satan.

In the midst of it all,

Learning how to take your time,

Not rushing;

Instead,

Learning how to be patient,

Recognizing it gets greater later

When you become grateful for right now.

Appreciating your ups and downs,

Staying encouraged,

While this world's evil ways

Will leave you discouraged;

Left in a predicament

Of being lost,
As I pray you will soon be found
Finding balance
To live a purposeful life
Of peace, love, and light.
Now get on the good foot,
Or should I say, good feet,
And get right on your balance.

message

Many are called;
Only a few are chosen.
Now who's to say
You are not a chosen one?
Look deep beneath the surface
And you will soon find your purpose,
Then you will realize the life you live
Is well worth it.
We all have unique qualities and differences
And something to live for,
With gifts so amazing
They're worth dying for.
Never sell yourself short,
There's a bigger plan

For you.

Never question

What the Almighty will do for you.

Trust and stay in pursuit of your happiness.

The words I wrote,

I pray you grasp a bit

And let them stick to your mind and spirit.

It's all ghetto gospel;

No, I am not an apostle.

Just a server created in the image

Of excellence,

Speaking for those

In the need of inspiration

In our village.

These gifts I have are a privilege

I have been blessed with.

I hope you receive a message.

You can quote anything I write

'Cause when you speak it,

The people gon' feel it.

They will recognize the truth

Through the words of

Tom Ray's Ghetto Gospel.

PEACE!

- You'll begin to understand more when you silence your mind and collect your scattered thoughts.

- The government is not going to change a thing; it will be God's divine and assigned people who will.

- As a young one, I wanted to be like Mike until I realized that imitation was subtracting from the fullest degree of my own potential. **BE YOU AND BE GREAT! SUCCESS IS THE MISSION.**

- It's not the enemy; it's the inner me. Give Satan no credit, family.

- **Pay attention:** Every righteous spirit is not adorned in godly garments; and not every demonic spirit is dressed in red with a two-horned headpiece.

- Show gratitude for life every day; and take nothing for granted — good or bad. Our plans compared to what God has in store for us will cause the Creator to laugh. We have a greater purpose; we are not worthless. Those who have faith and determination and can ignore distractions will always prosper.

- My mama's famous words, "Life is what you make it," so make it marvelous! **BE VICTORIOUS.**

- The doors have been opened. We only need to choose the right path to walk through them. Ironically, sometimes even our wrong choices lead us to that path.

- Trouble can lead to transformation when we assume accountability, face our trials head-on, and have a sincere desire to do better.

- The problem's not always the seed — check the soil.

- You have to go through a season of drought to understand harvest.

A peaceful heart leads to a healthy life; and **PURPOSE IS PARAMOUNT!!!!**

Growing up in the hood, messages emerge in everything — a bottle, a bullet, a fortune cookie, in music, on television, and most certainly on social media. The one place that is overlooked is in a **BOOK!**

We need to learn to listen, to understand, love to love, learn to forgive, and release grudges so we don't miss the blessings that come with the process of becoming self-aware. Take me at my word as I release encouragement through *The Thoughts of Ray.*

When going through life's ups and downs, the best thing we can do is pray to make it through the night and see the makings of a brighter day. Good night. Good morning!

* * * * * *

The Thoughts Of Ray, The Sequel —

Along this journey, I've realized how much power our queens possess. Queens, you are the definition of beauty — souls filled with love, wisdom, and an inner glow you maintain as your sworn duty.

The comfort and support you provide for a man is needful and divine; and while we can be a pain in the backside at times and make tons of mistakes, we deeply appreciate when you take the time to speak to us as only a woman could; as only a mother would. You hold us accountable in a most gracious way with understanding, forgiveness, tough love, and agape.

When a man finds a godly woman;

He has found a good thing.

See, Mama said

A long time ago,

If you don't have anything nice to say;

Don't say anything at all —

And she was right.

She also stated,

"Listen to understand

And don't get defensive."

See, Mama is wise

And she understands the power of words.

She knew when to be quiet too,

Shhh, 'cause silence is golden.

Remaining silent says a lot more than you think.

Then she said fervently,

"Speak some positivity into your life, chile,

'Cause an arsenal of a negative vocabulary

Will land you six-feet deep in a cemetery."

There's power in the tongue.

You can speak your death into reality

Or speak all that you want into existence —

You choose.

After all that, she said,

"Words hurt too."

Kids are a prime example of that.

Let a kid say to another child,

Your mama is this or that;

There's usually a physical reaction as payback,

While tears are pouring down their faces,

Saying everything they don't mean

Because they are not thinking before they speak;

Displaying what they saw

From their parents

Arguing and fighting last week;

And it all stems from

What Mama said in the beginning

Of the conversation,

"If you don't have anything nice to say,

Don't say anything at all."

Then she proceeded to

Sipping her tea and minding her business,

And you know God is her witness.

In her final words,

She said, "You baby,

You going to take all;

I told you to encourage the world

With your vision."

And the loved one said,

"SUCCESS IS THE MISSION!"

wise words from mama

You see, Mama is full of knowledge, with a couple of semesters of college under her belt; and earned a degree in wisdom from her experiences and struggles. She sought God above everyone else but often looked back and drew strength from the woes of our ancestors.

Then she read a poem to her grandchild entitled,

hey, angry young world

Baby,

It's not that bad;

Put a smile on your face!

Mean-mugging is ugly,

And you are beautiful | handsome.

What you are going through,

Only God knows;

Trust and believe

God won't give you anything

You can't handle.

Your situation can definitely

Be worse;

You're fortunate to have them.

Jordan's on your feet,

And diamonds in that third world country

You know nothing about

Got nothing on hers;

Walking on rocks, mud,

Things you can't imagine;

Her brother is too.

So listen, loved one,

You don't have to be that angry.

Anger leads to stress

And stress lowers your immune system.

Plus more…

You can still live a satisfying life

If your family is poor.

Money isn't everything;

Attitude is most important.

It will bring you fortune

On the flipside.

Thank your mother

Because you could have been aborted,

So that anger isn't worth it.

Pause on the attitude;

Instead show gratitude.

Even when you think you are not

Caught in your feelings,

Your body language shows

When you are being cruel.

Cheer up!

It really isn't as bad

As you think.

You better learn to

Enjoy life and be grateful

And stay afloat

Before you sink;

Because if you can't swim,

You're bound to

Drizzound,

Angry young world!!!!!!!!!!!!!!

I have been an educator in the Yonkers Public School District and program coordinator at the Nepperhan Community Center for more than ten years. I discovered that the anger displayed in a lot of our children stems from broken homes, minimal support, neglect, and the absence of a father.

Realistically, we know these factors lead to the results televised and publicized, all for a dollar sign. I didn't write this to tag along with the backlash of absentee fathers but acknowledge all fathers with present involvement. I know many who step up to the plate and knock it out the park for the young ones.

Salute, fellas!

happy fathers' day

We have
Come to the time
Of the year
When all fathers
Get recognized.
Whether good or bad,
Present or absent,
Your role as a provider, pops
Is not by accident.
Continue to strive
To be the best father
You can be.
You are a major
Necessity
To the stability of a family.
Homes are broken without you;
Sons are lost without you,
And daughters love to brag
About their first true love.
Mothers just want to be
Held in your arms
With a strong hug.
You are all appreciated —
Stepdads,

Thoughts of Ray, The Sequel

Godfathers,

Uncles who play the role of a father,

Grandfathers,

And fathers who are no longer with us.

(Sleep in peace, Pops; love and miss you!)

We pour a little libation

For your existence;

And pops,

If it's not right

With your child's mother,

Your seed is your

Number one commitment.

Remember,

They didn't ask to be here.

Your duties as a provider, pops,

Is recommended all year.

Today you are

Awarded;

Enjoy your gifts,

Pop your collar,

And continue to be

The father

Who knows

Time spent is worth more than a dollar.

HAPPY FATHERS' DAY!

You can't mention the father without mentioning the mother —
the queen, his rib and soul mate.

happy mother's day

Ladies,

Queens of the earth,

The mothers of sons and daughters —

You are everything and more.

We need you

Like we need water.

Every one of you is appreciated.

You are the topic of this

Poetic conversation.

You are God's greatest creation.

Life is birthed through you,

We come from you,

Beauty is inside you,

And when your baby is born,

We might roam for a while,

But we come back to find you.

Our first love,

Our nurturer;

The one woman that is going to

Ride with us,

Whether right or wrong,

Expressing that agape love —

Tough love,

Understanding and forgiving love.

You are a queen,

And we praise you;

We thank you

For laboring for nine months

To a life sentence

Of being about your child's business.

Our heavenly Father knew

What he was doing when

He made you a mother,

And it might not have been in your plan

As early.

I want to take the time

To remind you,

You are so worthy

Of royal acknowledgment

Every day, Queen;

Not just on Mother's Day,

We honor you everyday,

And I hope you are encouraged

By *The Thoughts of Ray.*

Now get your shine on

Like the sun in the month of May;

Sporting your favorite sundress,

Sitting back, getting some good rest;

Enjoying your flowers

While you can

Still smell them;

Smiling from cheek to cheek

Because that's how it's supposed to be,

Queen.

I'm going to remind you again,

You are royalty.

Value that beautiful black skin.

I salute each and every

One of you;

I give thanks because

BLACK WOMEN ROCK!

HAPPY MOTHER'S DAY.

* * * * * *

The Thoughts Of Ray, The Sequel —

Note to self and you:

You are too valuable to just exist.

Live life abundantly and with purpose!

message

To every mother, angry child, and father —

Loved ones,

Learn to sincerely let go

Of what you think you control

And seek healing from

The Son

Who will break the chains

Of your strongholds.

I'm not talking religion,

Within spirituality;

There's a difference.

The walk of faith is far from

Easy;

Sometimes the tests we face

That are disguised to stress us,

In all reality —

Every trial we endure

Is designed to bless us.

So worry less,

Learn to confess;

Fill that organ

With love

That's in the center of your chest.

Release that fear

Because the strong are going to always

Persevere;

And you are not finished yet!!!!!!!

SUCCESS IS THE MISSION.

★★★★★

While writing this book, I've been on a journey to obtain a better relationship with God on a personal level. Years before I wrote my first poetry novel, *The Thoughts of Ray from My Heart to Yours*, I attended church frequently and read the bible during the time of my college coursework. I thank God for my father who encouraged me to get up on Sunday mornings and attend service with him, even when I was tired from being out partying the night before.

Sometimes I went and other times I didn't, but when I did, it felt good to sit with my father and hear the word, although it didn't resonate with me very often. As a result, I neglected to attend at all for a while. Always a student, however, I was still open-minded to learning God's ways and seeking knowledge of self. A few years later, after my father passed away, I isolated myself and began to pray and spend time in silent reflection.

My cousin, JJ, invited me to attend service at City Refuge Christian Center (CRCC). My spirit was ignited by the spiritual teachings of Bishop Tracy Holloman, and soon thereafter, CRCC became my home church. Please don't get me wrong, I respect every religion, but I love God so much that love became the conviction of my faith. God is love, and we were created from His love where there is ...

greatness

That greatness that you are striving for,

Destined for.

We were created in it;

Alignment is the assignment

To finding it.

We are victorious.

We are God's warriors.

So get ready

For them war scars,

Beloved.

Yeah, it's a fact that

We come from the dirt,

But it's flavor

When we're rising above it together —

Unifying the masses,

Building the kingdom,

Cleansing our temples,

Feeding our mental,

And stacking our credentials;

Buying and skipping past a rental,

Recognizing the bigger picture.

Worrying less,

Accepting the fact that we are BLESSED;

Appreciating every breath

Of fresh air,

Giving flowers to our loved ones

While they can still smell them;

Now that's gratitude.

Mind over matter is the only thing

That matters,

Dude,

And queen,

You are beautiful.

King,

You are magnificent.

Don't Let no one

Tell you different.

You are uniquely made

With creative juices.

You got to add

Your own flavor;

Make your own concoction

And own it.

That's you,

Be you;

Not them.

There isn't a life

That is better than yours;

Comparison is a thief of joy.

Appreciate your genetic makeup.

There will never be another you.

That's what makes you great.

The life you live wouldn't be so adventurous

Without the mistakes you make;

And it takes a lot of time and patience

To master the art of being great.

Now before you get all bent out of shape,

Trying to be something you

Already are,

Be mindful of this —

You were created in the image of greatness,

Beloved.

Now step into your greatness

And be just that,

GREAT!

Tony the Tiger

Great!

That's a little throwback for you!

Let's take it back — a brief moment in time

I'll never forget,

I was that same kid

Wiling out to that Lox track;

And at the same time fronting in the mirror

Like I had a six-pack,

While brushing my waves;

You know I had to keep a wave cap.

And I got an ole soul,

My peers tell me.

I remind them of someone from way back,

Standing on the shoulders of the Panthers,

Yeah,

You know I'm pro-black;

And the only thing white

I ever moved was some Ajax.

Dog,

I come from the era,

If the music was trash,

You couldn't play that;

And if you ever invited someone

To the frank stand,

You'd better been ready to scrap,

And it wasn't a game

If you had to pull out the strap;

Years ago we were able

To communicate before it resulted to that.

Meanwhile…

I'm at the sneaker store,

Trying to cop them Jordans —

Patent leather,

White and black,

But I got the black and red.

Then I got the space jams,

Yeah,

I thought I was the man;

I've never been interested in

Peter Pan.

I had to figure out what I wanted to do

After seeing my brother

Flipping grams,

Then doing time served

by Uncle Sam;

Later on caught up in a jam

Just to put some food on the table

For the fam.

I'm highly grateful

Of becoming aware

Of who I truly am —

A FIGURE OF BLACK EXCELLENCE!

* * * * *

Speaking of nostalgia...

In the famous words

Of Michael Jackson,

The king of pop,

Do you

Remember the time when

Mannerism was not

Considered flattery,

And communicating was more

Of verbal conversation

Rather than a text

From a mobile device?

Better yet,

Do you remember

When you could pay

$1.50 for a slice,

And get a bundle of something nice

For the right price?

Whatever you like.

Man,

I remember when community block parties

Was rocking all day and night

With not a cop in sight.

We govern our own,

And wherever Pops

Left his hat was his home —

O.G. was a rolling stone.

And if Mama gave you a curfew,

Whatever time it was,

Your behind

Had better been home.

Those were the days;

And in the words of the pastor,

We in our last days,

So we got to give God all the praise.

We got to DO THE RIGHT THING!

And to all you crooked cops,

Stop doing my brothers like

Radio Raheem.

We just want some brothers on the wall.

We do more than

Rapping and playing ball.

Check it y'all!

Remember when Now and Laters were

Ten cents, y'all,

And Laffy Taffy was five cents?

This inflation,

Man,

It doesn't make sense.

Good times like that

Is what makes me reminisce.

Like,

When we were black and proud,

And the village raised the child;

Rakim moved the crowd,

Boom boxes were played loud,

And high-top fades were the style.

There were no cell phones back then;

You had to spin the nob before you dialed.

This was the Reagan era,

The Golden era,

The first snap-back era;

Fam, I remember

When Sauconys were twenty-five dollars.

Fellas,

Remember when we used

To write love letters, trying to holla,

And B-boys rocked

Gucci and Prada?

And for the ladies,

5411s with the strap across the top

Were the hottest shoe

On the block?

And…

Convertible drop tops

Turned heads right on the spot,

And the fire hydrant was the neighborhood pool?

You were not getting in

If you didn't do good in school,

Because Mama didn't raise no fool.

Ayo, do you remember when you could

Discipline your child

Without

CPS getting involved,

And sense was common,

Respecting elders

Was a must,

$1.75 or less would get you a ride on the bus,

$1.69 would get you a gallon of gas?

Man,

Don't you wish

We could flash back to the past

When all this trash music didn't get a pass?

I guess it's the sign of the times;

Reflecting off a dope past

Is the only time we should look behind.

In my closing words,

I'd like to propose a question…

do you remember the time?

This portion of the book is dedicated to all my brothers of color reppin' black culture. — Peace!

To every brother across the world of African descent,

Here's a message for you —

Heaven sent.

God didn't instill in you

A heart of fear,

Be fearless!

You're destined for greatness, king!

Yes, there are lots of odds and hate against you;

Let that inspire you

To feed your mental.

Nothing can stop an educated mind —

Not a thing.

Our mission

Started from a dream

And a will to succeed;

Putting in that work,

Gardening a fresh harvest,

And watering the seed.

We gon' make it, king.

You just gotta believe,
While having faith the size
Of a mustard seed;
More like a watermelon seed —
You know we black.
I'm just embracing the culture;
Being my brothers' keeper
Like I'm supposed to;
Writing and reciting,
Encouraging,
Enlightening,
For all my brothers
That are already under a
Concealed indictment
For nothing.
While you begin to get hated on,
Make sure you love yourself
Because that hate has nothing to do with you.
Godbody,
America filthy,
And we are not from here;
But while we're here,
We are not going anywhere
But to the mountaintop,
Vibrating higher,

Achieving in all our desires,

Staying inspired;

And staying out the way,

Praying and working toward

A better day;

Maintaining our inner peace,

Protecting our spirit

From the demonic force;

Loving yourself,

Building your community,

Not destroying it.

Respecting and appreciating our Queens,

Monitoring our health —

Good health is wealth

While becoming aware of knowledge of self.

We kings,

Fellas,

So let's step into our greatness

And show these young men

How an authentic man

Carries himself;

And the first of many steps

Is picking your pants up!

black man!

one month isn't enough

Black Excellence,

Black History —

According to the calendar,

We get one month a year.

To our recollection,

Our history is all year long —

Infinite.

The first,

Every day of our lives;

Don't settle for twenty-eight days.

Represent and honor

Our rich culture

For as long as you live.

Our ancestors

Should never

Go unrecognized for

All the fighting they did.

That's why one month isn't enough

Compared to our struggle.

We still fighting,

Waking up

From the lies,

Seeking divine

Enlightenment,

Reconnecting with family,

Loving thyself,

Restoring true principles

In our communities;

Governing our own.

This land is ours,

So wherever

We stand or live is where we belong.

Stand strong, loved ones,

Don't fold.

We got the power,

The numbers,

And we don't crack.

The representation

Of the black fist in the air

Symbolizes that

We are proud to be BLACK!

Because black is beautiful,

Black is pure and solid;

Golden,

Royal,

Immaculate,

Extravagant,

And more than just a color —

It's a lifestyle,

A culture

Full of riches

Coming from the motherland.

These are wise words written

In black

From your brother man.

Peace sister,

You are beautiful

And brother,

You a king.

Our ancestors told us

To believe in our dreams.

They also mentioned

Black don't crack,

And that's a well-known fact.

So you can't tell me

Black isn't beautiful.

We are godly;

Created in the image of greatness

And destined to shine

Like a black diamond

Draped in black onyx,

Suited in all black

With a beautiful,

Black queen by our side.

Standing strong and proud,

Full of pride;

And take a wild guess

On what kind of car she drives?

(take a wild guess)—

A black Cadillac Eldorado

Draped with black guts.

Black is beautiful;

Black is us;

Black is Excellent!

black excellence!

* * * * *

The Thoughts Of Ray, The Sequel —

Before I continue, I want to thank each of you for the overwhelming love, encouragement, and support received toward the development of this literary masterpiece. Every word expressed came from within and operates in agape inspired by the Most High, the first source of love.

While we continue to hope endlessly to see a brighter day, our contribution begins with setting a proper example for our young ones. Promote positivity, do good because it's right to do, take responsibility, speak truth, hold to accountability even in wrongdoing, remain humble when just, and encourage all ethnicities to unite. We are all one, right?

In the midst of all the madness on display in this world, divine work must be on the agenda because it will outlive time. The scenarios that occurred in the past are happening again in real time. The only difference now is that they are being televised. While there's nothing new under the sun, it is a new day, with new reflections captured on paper in this sequel to *THE THOUGHTS OF RAY.*

Beloved, you are a gift to this world, so stay encouraged. Seek knowledge of who you are within and let God heal the wounds life inflicted. Trials and tribulations serve a hidden purpose; and they build fortitude and character for greatness. You are an overcomer and will stand victorious.

God spoke through me as I penned the words to every poem and every message. As the saying goes, **"EACH ONE TEACH ONE,"** so I believe it's my responsibility to pass along every nugget of knowledge and wisdom I collect on this journey. I pray you embrace every word along with the intention to inspire embedded in every verse. In an attempt to understand the adversity we face, let me be the first to confess that the longsuffering we endure is a test of our faith and builds endurance to complete the race.

This journey is far from easy; it will never be, but the outcome will be far greater than the onset. I consider my passage to be an excellent testimony of how what we go through is working toward purpose. Choices we make can either become hindrances or fuel. The road to an abundant life will never be paved in perfection, but the lessons learned along the way equate to blessings; and what we go through is a worthwhile investment. Believe it or not, God is alongside us every step of the way, and to coin a verse — **faith without action is dead.**

That's why I have to shout out

The meek and the humble

Because

We shall inherit the earth.

Those dreams and nightmares you face

All serve a purpose;

And you my friend,

You've been victorious

Since your mother gave birth.

The lies we been fed

Done something to our appetite

To digest the truth.

We rather fast food,

And when we begin to wake up,

We become aware of the dangers of soul food.

Balance it all out in moderation;

In order to reach our

Highest potential in life,

Our old life and new life

Need some separation,

And you better learn some patience.

We be rushing to do everything,

And none of us are Russian.

I do know one thing —

You won't eat

If you not hustling.

That's universal language written in braille;

Without confessing to our strong holds

How do you expect to heal?

Now that's true conviction,

With all due respect to every Christian,

Love is my religion;

And my heart ninety percent pure,

Because none of us are one hundred percent righteous,

On the real!

It took a whole lot of courage just to write this,

But with this gift

God blessed me with,

I will forever write and recite.

For my loved ones

Seeking enlightenment —

As you can see,

"Each one teach one"

Is one of my favorite mottos;

And I'll leave you with this

One last thing:

Please don't mistake

The Thoughts of Ray

For a message in a bottle -

This is a poetic gospel.

SUCCESS IS THE MISSION!

To all of my family and loved ones, I love each and every one of you with all my heart. We gon' make it. Bless up!

The Thoughts of Ray —

One summer morning, I woke up with a strong impression upon my heart to write this poetry novel.

Adversely, I felt a heavy burden and was mentally drained due to the crisis of our brothers being murdered by their own in the street over nonsense.

Yes, police brutality and unjustified hate crimes are televised on a daily basis; but in our own communities, we are gunning each other down and falling right into the devil's plan like it's the right thing to do.

Yes, protect yourself, loved ones, but the ignorance needs to stop. We can protest, rally, and march to stop the oppressors from killing us; and while I don't condemn those strategies, what about **US KILLING US?** Remember, two wrongs never made anything right. Now I am speaking to those who boast about bussing guns. Learn how to communicate, and if you get punched in the face, learn how to fight. Statistically, we will continue to fill up jails, bury mothers' children, and keep the Willie Lynch letters relevant if we do not **CHANGE** our ways!

It's time to love ourselves and value life. Before picking up a pistol, think about how much life will be served behind bars under the authority of the prison system. There was a time when we settled matters with a good ole fistfight and a talk afterward. We have lost far too many great human beings to gun violence. That's a fact!

Now correct me if I'm wrong,

Since when

Has it been cool

To glorify

Being a gangster?

Better yet,

Since when has killing someone

Or promoting gun violence

Been cool?

In my opinion,

I don't have a clue;

For all those that do,

With all due respect,

Start holding yourself

Accountable

For what you represent.

I'm not pointing

Any fingers;

I'm just stating the truth;

Doing what a lot of folks

Claim they do.

FACTS —

These concrete streets

Don't kill people,

Soulless people do,

Misguided people do,

Uneducated people do.

I pray you allow

God to reach you

Before it is too late…

Receiving that

Open invitation

To hell

Or them pearly gates.

Truth be told,

We're all going to make mistakes.

There's no excuse for all this gun violence;

Continuous crime against crime.

I don't even want to speak on

Police brutality

Because that's nothing new.

For those of you in the hood,

Ghettos, and projects,

Across the world,

I'm speaking to each and every one of you.

You want change,

Change yourself.

Set a better example

For these kids

Watching you,

Because that's where it starts

With their pure hearts;

Their hearts are not corrupt,

At least not yet,

Nor do they know what

Racism is.

They full of love,

Or looking for it,

Just like these

Self-acclaimed

Thugs, gangsters, shooters,

And misled adolescents.

All the lessons

That present themselves

In your life

Are disguised blessings

For you to get closer to the One

Who isn't going to

Tell anyone during a confession.

Stop killing

Each other,

Loved ones,

We just falling

Right into the oppressor's plan.

We need peace on this land;

We need one another;

We need for every one of us

To start

Holding

Ourselves accountable

For our own mistakes,

For our own wrongs;

We need every ethnicity

To get along.

We need to stop

Hating each other,

Killing each other,

And learn to understand one another;

And to see the next man as our brother,

No matter the color!

I can't write it enough,

We need to love one another

Or you know the rest —

I pray for every one of your

Loved ones to have the best in abundance.

WE ARE ONE!

thank you***

Love is the strongest vibration, the spark to ignite change.
Love yourself and then you you'll understand what it means
to love another.

But
NAH, SON,
Mama twerking,
Her daughter twerking;
Pops not working
And got the nerve
To be in the club;
Milly rocking;
And
The son's eighteen,
And he's an O.G.
From
Licking shots on the block
At his
Own kind.
How sway?
It blows my mind,
The chaos
From the blind
Leading the blind.

I'm just venting
From what I see;
Mentally,
I pray for all my loved ones
In every community.
I don't blame us
To the full capacity,
Because we have been
Condemned in captivity
For centuries.
Screw the excuses, though,
I know we can do better.
The question is,
Do we want to do better
Or just stay stagnated?
Complaining about
The choices we make;
Refusing to hold
Ourselves accountable
For our own horse manure.
NAH, SON,
It doesn't work like that.
Change requires
Making a good choice,
Doing the right thing,

Putting order to our steps,

Loving our neighbor,

Being grateful for Gods favor,

Getting things done now

Not later;

Taking care of mother earth,

Men not dressings in skirts,

Women knowing their self-worth,

With both parents being present

At their child's birth.

And we can all front…

But NAH, SON,

We all been hurt,

Seeking healing,

In the wrong places,

Deceived by smiles on crooked faces;

Praying for justice to be served

In corrupt cases.

In order

For life to become

Less complex,

We got to get back to the basics.

But nah,

The fundamentals get ignored now —

Like displaying

Manners, morals,

Self-respect, self-love —

Having the ability to listen

Without becoming defensive;

Staying true to our commitments,

While having the patience,

Consistence, and persistence,

To go the distance.

We be too busy rushing;

Moving in a NY minute.

NAH, BELOVED,

Take your time;

Master the process.

Cultivate your mojo,

Get the fear out your heart.

Face the adversity;

Stop running.

Give Satan no credit;

All praises due to Allah!

Inshallah,

That we make it to tomorrow.

Am I Muslim?

NAH, SON,

Just a messenger

On the mission;

Destined to get the job done;

Speaking for the voiceless

Who reside where I come from.

We gon' make it, y'all!

It was already written.

So ignore every single thought

Of quitting,

Loved one,

Because so they say,

We born to lose,

But

You know what we gon' tell them?

benediction

NAH, SON,

The fight don't stop!

Since the beginning of time and for as long as I can remember, physical altercations, mental frustration, and war has been in the forefront of this country's news and plastered on television screens.

As children, we were taught if someone hits you, hit them back; and as adults, we still struggle with the choice to respond *(communicate)* or fight *(react)*. Self-defense, there's nothing wrong with that, but fighting over territory that we don't own has become first nature; and the fight has become the norm.

Now we fight over misunderstandings, for notoriety, and sometimes we even fight against reaching the fullest potential and purpose in ourselves — all due to mental chaos and scattered thoughts.

We often struggle with our past while striving for a better future in response to all the turbulence we been through. We scrap for a slice of the pie when there's enough for everyone to eat. Fighting over he said, she said — the root cause of many confrontations in the street. Some fight to resolve symptoms of depression, and at this very moment, **SOMEONE IS FIGHTING TO STAY ALIVE**, while the nation's activists are fighting for equal justice for Black Lives.

THE FIGHT DON'T STOP!

Every day, it's a battle

In the jungle for

Our souls

And warfare

Against

Spiritual principalities.

What was once simple,

Turned into technicalities;

And all types of assaults and batteries

Every night in the hood.

Turn on the news

The morning after

There's a tragedy;

This is the confession
Of a harsh reality;
Kids killing kids is total insanity.
We still fighting for the day
To see the standards of
Equal humanity…
And it's supposed to be the land of the free;
Well,
Not for those
The same shade as me.
The times we in now
Make you honor
And appreciate
Our ancestors' legacy.
The adversity we face
Is just a test
To our destiny.
One day,
You will be asked,
What did you do
To help the oppressed?
Did you lend a helping hand,
Or are you battling from the lack of
Self-love and mis-education,
Fighting to establish

A lucrative occupation?
The sad thing about it is,
Someone on the same path as you
Is probably hating;
Now you are fighting,
Debating
Whether to go crazy
Or stay sane.
The funny thing
About the ongoing fight is,
When you recognize
How blessed you are
And whose side you're on,
You won't complain;
You become grateful
Of your hardships.
It builds character,
Endurance,
Tenacity;
Every doubtful thought
In your mind
Is total blasphemy;
Completely false
To God's plan for us.
We are born

VICTORIOUS

With a purpose,

To produce good in this world;

And as soon as we come out the womb,

We fighting off

Deadly medications;

Those mentally woke

Comprehend what I'm saying.

We fight from birth,

Fighting to stay alive…

For decades we have been

Fighting our own kind

With poor explanations

To explain why.

In most cases,

The initial complications

Start in the mind,

Fighting to maintain

That inner peace.

Along the journey,

I learned

There's power in calmness,

To say the least.

Nah, the fight don't stop,

But

What's better than

Words of encouragement

As one of your techniques

To fight off the beast?

The truth of the word

Is the only thing

That's going to last —

The lies, doubts,

Fears, insecurities,

And plot of our

Downfall is obsolete.

The Thoughts of Ray

Was written to honor

God

And inspire more world peace.

So as you continue on,

Loved one,

Stay solid,

Don't fold,

Or lose faith.

PEACE!!!

Thank you all for genuine and actionable support.

Peace, family!

— Ray

conclusion
SUCCESS IS THE MISSION*

As we conclude, I hope this read has left you inspired, encouraged, and provoked in thought. Before I published my first poetry novel, I was in the process of recording an extended play (EP) — my brothers, OC and Mark Ware, are my witnesses.

I was, however, rerouted creatively to author two literary pieces, *The Thoughts of Ray from My Heart to Yours* and *P.A.I.N.* This sequel of The Thoughts of Ray is the third phase of the project, and God gets all the honor.

While cultivating my spoken word gift, I was often asked, *"Ray when are you going to record and produce your poems?"* There is no time like the present. Tune in to The Thoughts of Ray on all streaming platforms and watch for upcoming audio books and soundtracks!

Thank you all for genuine and actionable support.

Peace, family!

— Ray